Death Comes to the War Poets

Other Works of Interest from St. Augustine's Press

Joseph Pearce, *Beauteous Truth:*
Faith, Reason, Literature and Culture
James V. Schall, S.J., *The Regensburg Lecture*
James V. Schall, S.J., *Modern Age*
James V. Schall, S.J., *The Classical Moment*
James V. Schall, S.J., *The Sum Total of Human Happiness*
James V. Schall, S.J., *Remembering Belloc*
Marc D. Guerra, ed., *Jesursalem, Athens, and Rome:*
Essays in Honor of James V. Schall, S.J.
Kenneth Baker, S.J., *Jesus Christ – True God and True Man*
Ernest Fortin, A.A., *Christianity and Philosophical Culture*
in the Fifth Century
Servais Pinckaers, O.P., *Morality: The Catholic View*
Rémi Brague, *On the God of the Christians*
(and on one or two others)
Richard Peddicord, O.P., *The Sacred Monster of Thomism:*
An Introduction to the Life and Legacy of Garrigou-Lagrange, O.P.
Josef Pieper and Heinz Raskop, *What Catholics Believe*
Josef Pieper, *Happiness and Contemplation*
Peter Geach, *God and the Soul*
Gabriel Marcel, *Man against Mass Society*
Dietrich von Hildebrand, *The Heart*
Robert Hugh Benson, *Lord of the World*
Peter Kreeft, *The Philosophy of Jesus*
Peter Kreeft, *Jesus-Shock*
Philippe Bénéton, *The Kingdom Sufferth Violence:*
The Machiavelli / Erasmus / More Correspondence
H.S. Gerdil, *The Anti-Emile: Reflections on the Theory and Practice*
of Education against the Principles of Rousseau
Edward Feser, *The Last Superstition:*
A Reflection on the New Atheism
Roger Kimball, *The Fortunes of Permanence:*
Culture and Anarchy in an Age of Amnesia
George William Rutler, *Principalities and Powers:*
Spiritual Combat 1942–1943

Death Comes to the War Poets
A Verse Tapestry

Being a Dramatic Presentation of the Poetry of Siegfried
Sassoon and Wilfred Owen, with cameo appearances
by Thomas Gray, Gerard Manley Hopkins, T. S. Eliot,
G. K. Chesterton, Rupert Brooke, Edith Sitwell,
and Joseph Pearce

Arranged for dramatic and narrative effect by
Joseph Pearce

St. Augustine's Press
South Bend, Indiana

Manufactured in the United States of America.

1 2 3 4 5 6 24 23 22 21 20 19 18 17

Library of Congress Cataloging in Publication Data
Library of Congress Control Number: 2017938394

∞ The paper used in this publication meets the minimum requirements of the American National Standard for Information Sciences – Permanence of Paper for Printed Materials, ANSI Z39.48-1984.

St. Augustine's Press
www.staugustine.net

Table of Contents

Setting the Scene

The following verse tapestry, being a dramatic presentation of the poetry of Siegfried Sassoon, Wilfred Owen and others, has been woven in commemoration and celebration of five anniversaries that fall in this year of 2017. First, we commemorate the centenary, in April 2017, of the entry of the United States into World War One; second, we commemorate, in July 2017, the centenary of the publication of Siegfried Sassoon's "Soldier's Declaration"; third, we celebrate the centenary, later the same year, of the meeting of Sassoon with his fellow war poet, Wilfred Owen, at Craiglockhart War Hospital; fourth, we commemorate the sixtieth anniversary of Sassoon's reception into the Catholic Church in September 1957; and finally, we commemorate the fiftieth anniversary of Sassoon's death in September 1967.

Like most of the great poets, Siegfried Sassoon is not as well known today as he ought to be. This verse tapestry is, therefore, intended as a timely tribute to a writer who deserves to be more widely known, not only for the acerbic gravitas of the war poetry for which he is best known but also for the poetry and prose that he wrote after the war.

Born in Kent, in south east England, in 1886, Sassoon's experience of the trenches of World War One embittered him. Although he fought with great courage, being awarded the Military Cross for gallantry in battle, he was angered by the conduct of the war and the wholesale slaughter that it unleashed. In a barrage of bitter invective, expressed in satirical verse which became very popular as the initial enthusiasm for the war began to wane, he vented his spleen against the politicians, journalists and senior military officers, whom he believed responsible for enflaming and prolonging the carnage. Typical of this astringent verse is "Suicide in the Trenches":

I knew a simple soldier boy
Who grinned at life in empty joy,
Slept soundly through the lonesome dark,
And whistled early with the lark.
In winter trenches, cowed and glum,
With crumps and lice and lack of rum,
He put a bullet through his brain.
No one spoke of him again.

You smug-faced crowds with kindling eye
Who cheer when soldier lads march by,
Sneak home and pray you'll never know
The hell where youth and laughter go.

In more prosaic fashion, his "Soldier's Declaration," addressed ostensibly to his commanding officer but published or quoted in several newspapers, was "an act of wilful defiance of military authority," condemning those in power for prolonging "the suffering of the troops . . . for ends which I believe to be evil and unjust." Having experienced the unspeakable horrors of trench warfare, Sassoon's "Declaration" also complained about "the callous complaisance with which the majority of those at home regard the continuance of the agonies which they do not share and have not sufficient imagination to realise."

In a further gesture of defiance, Sassoon threw his Military Cross into the River Mersey, and his notoriety reached new heights when his "Declaration" was read in the House of Commons. Faced with this open and very public defiance of the war effort, Sassoon was declared mentally overwrought and therefore not responsible for his actions. In true Orwellian fashion, he was confined to a military hospital in Scotland until he recovered his senses. It was here that he met and befriended Wilfred Owen, a poet who shared his anger at the war and who expressed it with the same vitriolic fervor.

Owen would be killed in action on November 4, 1918, only a week before the Armistice, one of the final victims of the dying embers of the war, a slaughtered lamb, butchered before his gifts could be developed. Sassoon, on the other hand, would live to a ripe old age.

After the war, Sassoon's reputation as a writer of first-rate prose, as well as poetry, was sealed with the publication of the three volume semi-fictitious autobiography, *The Complete Memoirs of George Sherston* (1937). In 1945, at the end of the second of the world wars which the century of "progress" had wrought, Sassoon's skepticism towards modernity and its vacuous promises was expressed with razor-sharp eloquence in "Litany of the Lost":

> In breaking of belief in human good;
> In slavedom of mankind to the machine;
> In havoc of hideous tyranny withstood,
> And terror of atomic doom foreseen;
> Deliver us from ourselves.
>
> Chained to the wheel of progress uncontrolled;
> World masterers with a foolish frightened face;
> Loud speakers, leaderless and sceptic-souled;
> Aeroplane angels, crashed from glory and grace;
> Deliver us from ourselves.
>
> In blood and bone contentiousness of nations,
> And commerce's competitive re-start,
> Armed with our marvellous monkey innovations,
> And unregenerate still in head and heart;
> Deliver us from ourselves.

As the world stumbled from world war to cold war, Sassoon befriended Father Ronald Knox whose *God and the Atom* had expressed the same post-traumatic stress in the wake of the dropping of the atom bombs on Hiroshima and Nagasaki as had Sassoon's "Litany of the

Lost." Knox died in August 1957 and, a month later, Sassoon was received into the Catholic Church, a few weeks after his seventy-first birthday and a full forty years after Knox's own conversion.

Following his conversion, Sassoon, the war poet, became a poet of peace, a fact expressed in the title of the first volume of poetry he published as a Catholic. *The Path to Peace*, published in 1960, was essentially an autobiography in verse, ranging from the earliest sonnets of his youth to the religious poetry of his last years. Of the latter, his long meditative poem, "Lenten Illuminations," written during his first Lent as a Catholic, is surely one of the finest Christian poems of the twentieth century, inviting comparisons with T. S. Eliot's "Ash Wednesday," which had also been written shortly after the poet's conversion. It is a monologue which the poet addresses to the ghost of his pre-convert self, musing on their life and how it had led him to his knees in a church:

> While you were in your purgatorial time,
>   you used to say
> That though Creation's God remained so lost,
>   such aeons away,
> Somehow He would reveal Himself to you—
>   some day!
> For Him, the Living God, your soul and flesh could
>   only cry aloud.
> In watches of the night, when world event with
>   devildom went dark,
> You implored illumination. But never being bowed

Obedient—never conceived an aureoled instance,
an assuring spark.

Apart from the brilliance of the poetry in its own right, shining forth as a visible witness to the good, the true and the beautiful, there is also a more prosaic and practical relevance to Sassoon's life and work. Having lived through two fratricidal world wars, fighting courageously in the first, and having become utterly disillusioned with the lifeless coldness of modern secular "progress," with which the world with devildom had gone dark, he had finally found the peace beyond all understanding which, as Eliot had discovered, was the only authentic escape from the wasteland of worldliness.

There is no better way to end a discussion of the greatness of Siegfried Sassoon, and to summarize the wisdom that he had gained after a life of suffering, than in his own words as poured forth in praise in "A Prayer in Old Age":

Bring no expectance of heaven unearned
No hunger for beatitude to be
Until the lesson of my life is learned
Through what Thou didst for me.

Bring no assurance of redeemed rest
No intimation of awarded grace
Only contrition, cleavingly confessed
To Thy forgiving face.

I ask one world of everlasting loss
In all I am, that other world to win.
My nothingness must kneel below Thy Cross.
There let new life begin.

Death Comes for the War Poets

A Verse Tapestry

Being a Dramatic Presentation of the Poetry of Siegfried Sassoon and Wilfred Owen, with cameo appearances by Thomas Gray, Gerard Manley Hopkins, T. S. Eliot, G. K. Chesterton, Rupert Brooke, Edith Sitwell, and Joseph Pearce Arranged for dramatic and narrative effect by Joseph Pearce

Dramatis Personae

Death, a female spirit

Siegfried Sassoon, Soldier and Poet

Wilfred Owen, Soldier and Poet

*Before the Curtain Rises, **DEATH** (off stage) sings a somber, haunting rendition of "Pack Up Your Troubles":*

Pack up your troubles in your old kit-bag,

And smile, smile, smile,

While you've a lucifer to light your fag,

Smile, boys, that's the style.

What's the use of worrying?

It never was worth while, so

Pack up your troubles in your old kit-bag,

And smile, smile, smile.

Enter SIEGFRIED SASSOON, wearing a heavy coat, looking youthful, spritely, carefree and every inch the young poet. He is shadowed by DEATH, looking hag-like, like one of the witches from Macbeth.

SASSOON:

OLD English songs, you bring to me

A simple sweetness somewhat kin

To birds that through the mystery

Of earliest morn make tuneful din,

While hamlet steeples sleepily

At cock-crow chime out three and four,

Till maids get up betime and go

With faces like the red sun low

Clattering about the dairy floor.

DEATH, ominously, portentously:

The curfew tolls the knell of parting day,

    The lowing herd wind slowly o'er the lea,

The plowman homeward plods his weary way,

    And leaves the world to darkness and to me.

SASSOON, merrily, cheerfully:
SHEPHERDS go whistling on their way

In the spring season of the year;

One watches weather-signs of day;

One of his maid most dear

Dreams; and they do not hear

The birds that sing and sing; they do not see

Wide wealds of blue beyond their windy lea,

Nor blossoms red and white on every tree.

DEATH, sneeringly, cynically:

Beneath those rugged elms, that yew-tree's shade,

    Where heaves the turf in many a mould'ring heap,

Each in his narrow cell for ever laid,

    The rude forefathers of the hamlet sleep.

The breezy call of incense-breathing Morn,

    The swallow twitt'ring from the straw-built shed,

The cock's shrill clarion, or the echoing horn,

No more shall rouse them from their lowly bed.

SASSOON, wide-eyed with innocence:

FOR Morn, my dome of blue,

For Meadows, green and gay,

And Birds who love the twilight of the leaves,

Let Jesus keep me joyful when I pray.

For the big Bees that hum

And hide in bells of flowers;

For the winding roads that come

To Evening's holy door,

May Jesus bring me grateful to his arms,

And guard my innocence for evermore.

DEATH, sneering:

The boast of heraldry, the pomp of pow'r,

    And all that beauty, all that wealth e'er gave,

Awaits alike th' inevitable hour.

    The paths of glory lead but to the grave.

Can storied urn or animated bust

    Back to its mansion call the fleeting breath?

Can Honour's voice provoke the silent dust,

    Or Flatt'ry soothe the dull cold ear of Death?

DEATH turns to address the audience:

"Some find me a sword; some

    The flange and the rail; flame,

Fang, or flood" goes Death on drum,

    And storms bugle my fame.

But you dréam you are rooted in earth—Dust!

Flesh falls within sight of us, you, though your flower
      the same,

Wave with the meadow, forget that there must

The sour scythe cringe, and the blear share come.

*[Siegfried Sassoon stands silently and still, as if in a trance.
Death turns towards him and addresses the following lines
to him. He stares straight ahead, not hearing her words.]*

Hope springs eternal on New Year's Day

Nineteen Fourteen,

And all sing *Auld Lang Syne*;

But Hell sings infernal songs (who hears, pray):

[Sings, to the tune of "My Love is Like a Red, Red Rose"]

"Till a' ye see's gangrene, my boys,

A' ye see's gangrene,

And I will have ye here, my boys,

Where a' ye see's gangrene."

Thus the red rose burns and has for thee

The subtle stench of blasphemy,

And bell's chime

Is Hell's crime

And the bell tolls for thee:

A virgin child,

So weak and wild,

A lamb to the slaughter;

Blinking blind,

Fumbling find

And kiss the devil's daughter.

[Kisses him. He does not respond. She continues to speak, as if hypnotizing him with auto-suggestive subliminal and subconscious seduction.]

If I should die, think only this of me:

That there's some corner of a foreign field

That is for ever England. There shall be

In that rich earth a richer dust concealed;

A dust whom England bore, shaped, made aware,

Gave, once, her flowers to love, her ways to roam,

A body of England's, breathing English air,

Washed by the rivers, blest by suns of home.

SASSOON awakes, as if from a dream, and speaks with naïve and youthful idealism, removing his heavy overcoat to reveal an army greatcoat underneath:

The anguish of the earth absolves our eyes

Till beauty shines in all that we can see.

War is our scourge; yet war has made us wise,

And, fighting for our freedom, we are free.

Horror of wounds and anger at the foe,

And loss of things desired; all these must pass.

We are the happy legion, for we know

Time's but a golden wind that shakes the grass.

There was an hour when we were loath to part

From life we longed to share no less than others.

Now, having claimed this heritage of heart,

What need we more, my comrades and my brothers?

DEATH, still unseen and unheard by Sassoon, sings with jingoistic jollity:

Pack up your troubles in your old kit-bag,

And smile, smile, smile,

While you've a lucifer to light your fag,

Smile, boys, that's the style.

What's the use of worrying?

It never was worth while, so

Pack up your troubles in your old kit-bag,

And smile, smile, smile. *[Steps aside, smirking cynically at Sassoon.]*

SASSOON:

GIVE me your hand, my brother, search my face;

Look in these eyes lest I should think of shame;

For we have made an end of all things base.

We are returning by the road we came.

Your lot is with the ghosts of soldiers dead,

And I am in the field where men must fight.

But in the gloom I see your laurell'd head

And through your victory I shall win the light.

DEATH:

A virgin child,

So weak and wild,

A lamb to the slaughter;

Blinking blind,

Fumbling find

And kiss the devil's daughter;

[Kisses him.]

A debutant dilettante,

Into Hell to follow Dante

And dance the deadly dance;

And so Sassoon,

So soon, Sassoon,

You join the necromance.

SASSOON, his face darkening:

THROUGH darkness curves a spume of falling flares

That flood the field with shallow, blanching light.

    The huddled sentry stares

    On gloom at war with white,

And white receding slow, submerged in gloom.

Guns into mimic thunder burst and boom,

And mirthless laughter rakes the whistling night.

The sentry keeps his watch where no one stirs

But the brown rats, the nimble scavengers.

DEATH:

And not

In fear, no

Inferno

Story worries you.

Bland!

See no evil,

Speak no evil,

Infer no evil:

Glory hurries you.

Blind!

SASSOON, increasingly angry:

THE Bishop tells us: "When the boys come back

They will not be the same; for they'll have fought

In a just cause: they lead the last attack

On Anti-Christ; their comrades' blood has bought

New right to breed an honourable race,

They have challenged Death and dared him face to
    face."

"We're none of us the same!" the boys reply.

"For George lost both his legs; and Bill's stone blind;

Poor Jim's shot through the lungs and like to die;

And Bert's gone syphilitic: you'll not find

A chap who's served that hasn't found some change."

And the Bishop said: "The ways of God are strange!"

[Pauses. Turns. Continues.]

I'D been on duty from two till four.

I went and stared at the dug-out door.

Down in the frowst I heard them snore.

"Stand to!" Somebody grunted and swore.

Dawn was misty; the skies were still;

Larks were singing, discordant, shrill;

They seemed happy; but I felt ill.

Deep in water I splashed my way

Up the trench to our bogged front line.

Rain had fallen the whole damned night.

O Jesus, send me a wound to-day,

And I'll believe in Your bread and wine,

And get my bloody old sins washed white!

DEATH:

So they cheered as you marched to war,

A jingo jangled cavalier,

But sneered the sign above the door:

"Abandon hope who enters here."

And so Sassoon,

So soon, Sassoon,

In nightmare you're awake

With senseless insommeniacs,

Marneiacs, La Monsiacs,

A sight fair for a wake.

SASSOON, walking forward and addressing the audience:

Enough is enough! No more! This butchery must end!

I, Second-Lieutenant Siegfried Sassoon of the Third Battalion Royal Welch Fusiliers, make this Soldier's Declaration to announce that I am finished with this war.

I am making this statement as an act of wilful defiance of military authority, because I believe that the war is being deliberately prolonged by those who have the power to end it.

}24{

I am a soldier, convinced that I am acting on behalf of soldiers. I believe that this war, upon which I entered as a war of defence and liberation, has now become a war of aggression and conquest. I believe that the purposes for which I and my fellow soldiers entered upon this war should have been so clearly stated as to have made it impossible to change them, and that, had this been done, the objects which actuated us would now be attainable by negotiation.

I have seen and endured the sufferings of the troops, and I can no longer be a party to prolong these sufferings for ends which I believe to be evil and unjust.

I am not protesting against the conduct of the war, but against the political errors and insecurities for which the fighting men are being sacrificed.

On behalf of those who are suffering now I make this protest against the deception which is being practiced on them; also I believe that I may help to destroy the callous complacence with which the majority of those at home regard the continuance of agonies which they do not share, and which they have not sufficient imagination to realize.

I declare, furthermore, that I do not make this declaration as a coward, as one who is afraid to fight for his country. On the contrary, I earned this Military Cross *[unpinning the medal from his chest and showing it forth]* for fighting with valour for my country. It means nothing to me now. Or rather, which is worse, it shames me to wear it, knowing how many have been butchered and are being butchered in my country's blood-spattered name. It shames me to wear this bloody bauble. It can go to the hell that it signifies. *[Casting the medal away, he steps to the back of the stage.]*

Enter WILFRED OWEN, speaking:

What passing-bells for these who die as cattle?

—Only the monstrous anger of the guns.

Only the stuttering rifles' rapid rattle

Can patter out their hasty orisons.

No mockeries now for them; no prayers nor bells;

Nor any voice of mourning save the choirs,—

The shrill, demented choirs of wailing shells;

And bugles calling for them from sad shires.

What candles may be held to speed them all?

Not in the hands of boys, but in their eyes

Shall shine the holy glimmers of goodbyes.

The pallor of girls' brows shall be their pall;

Their flowers the tenderness of patient minds,

And each slow dusk a drawing-down of blinds.

[Sassoon steps forward. The two men greet each other.]

OWEN: Lieutenant Sassoon, I believe. *[They shake hands.]* Owen. Wilfred Owen. Second Lieutenant, Manchester Regiment. It's a true honour to meet you.

SASSOON, laughing bitterly: An honour? I seem to be considered the most dishonourable of cads in most reputable circles.

OWEN: Only by those who are themselves dishonourable cads. I've not met a frontline soldier who disagrees with what you said.

SASSOON: But it wasn't said for the benefit of those who know the ugly truth but for those who don't know it, or don't want to know it, or refuse to know it.

OWEN: Well, you certainly let them have it. I thought you'd be shot after your Declaration was read in Parliament.

SASSOON: After the nightmare horror of the Somme, a firing squad would be nothing to fear. And yet, it seems, a firing squad is too good for me. So, evidently, is a good old-fashioned court martial. Instead they declare me sick in the head, sending me to this God-forsaken corner until I regain my senses. I'm declared to be as insane as these poor sods who have lost their minds in some bomb-blasted hellhole in France.

OWEN, visibly shaken: I fear that mine is lost in one of those hellholes . . . At least it was . . . For a while . . . I think I've found it again now . . . Or perhaps I'm just picking up the pieces . . . The fragments . . . All that's left of what once was me . . . Or what I thought was me . . . The rest of it is in the shell hole where I left it . . . Or where it was ripped from me . . . I was unconscious for a long time, you know . . . God knows how long . . . A trench mortar hit us . . . When I regained consciousness, I was lying next to the severed remains of a good friend . . . My best friend . . . A fellow officer . . . They picked up the pieces of his body and threw them together into a hole . . . The pieces of my severed self are still scattered . . . somewhere there where we lay together.

SASSOON, resting his arm on Owen's shoulder: I'm sorry, old man.

OWEN [turning away, deep in thought]:

He sat in a wheeled chair, waiting for dark,

And shivered in his ghastly suit of grey,

Legless, sewn short at elbow. Through the park

Voices of boys rang saddening like a hymn,

Voices of play and pleasure after day,

Till gathering sleep had mothered them from him.

About this time Town used to swing so gay

When glow-lamps budded in the light-blue trees

And girls glanced lovelier as the air grew dim,

—In the old times, before he threw away his knees.

Now he will never feel again how slim

Girls' waists are, or how warm their subtle hands,

All of them touch him like some queer disease.

There was an artist silly for his face,

For it was younger than his youth, last year.

Now he is old; his back will never brace;

He's lost his colour very far from here,

Poured it down shell-holes till the veins ran dry,

And half his lifetime lapsed in the hot race,

And leap of purple spurted from his thigh.

One time he liked a bloodsmear down his leg,

After the matches carried shoulder-high.

It was after football, when he'd drunk a peg,

He thought he'd better join. He wonders why . . .

Someone had said he'd look a god in kilts.

That's why; and maybe, too, to please his Meg,

Aye, that was it, to please the giddy jilts,

He asked to join. He didn't have to beg;

Smiling they wrote his lie; aged nineteen years.

Germans he scarcely thought of; and no fears

Of Fear came yet. He thought of jewelled hilts

For daggers in plaid socks; of smart salutes;

And care of arms; and leave; and pay arrears;

Esprit de corps; and hints for young recruits.

And soon, he was drafted out with drums and cheers.

DEATH:

So they cheered as you marched to war,

A jingo jangled cavalier,

But sneered the sign above the door:

"Abandon hope who enters here."

OWEN:

Some cheered him home, but not as crowds cheer Goal.

Only a solemn man who brought him fruits

Thanked him; and then inquired about his soul.

Now, he will spend a few sick years in Institutes,

And do what things the rules consider wise,

And take whatever pity they may dole.

Tonight he noticed how the women's eyes

Passed from him to the strong men that were whole.

How cold and late it is! Why don't they come

And put him into bed? Why don't they come?

SASSOON:

Propped on a stick he viewed the August weald;

Squat orchard trees and oasts with painted cowls;

A homely, tangled hedge, a corn-stalked field,

And sound of barking dogs and farmyard fowls.

And he'd come home again to find it more

Desirable than ever it was before.

How right it seemed that he should reach the span

Of comfortable years allowed to man!

Splendid to eat and sleep and choose a wife,

Safe with his wound, a citizen of life.

He hobbled blithely through the garden gate,

And thought: "Thank God they had to amputate!"

[Pauses. Turns. Continues.]

IF I were fierce, and bald, and short of breath,

    I'd live with scarlet Majors at the Base,

And speed glum heroes up the line to death.

    You'd see me with my puffy petulant face,

Guzzling and gulping in the best hotel,

    Reading the Roll of Honour. "Poor young chap,"

I'd say—"I used to know his father well;

    Yes, we've lost heavily in this last scrap."

And when the war is done and youth stone dead,

I'd toddle safely home and die—in bed.

[Pauses. Turns. Continues.]

"Good-morning, good-morning!" the General said

When we met him last week on our way to the line.

Now the soldiers he smiled at are most of 'em dead,

And we're cursing his staff for incompetent swine.

"He's a cheery old card," grunted Harry to Jack

As they slogged up to Arras with rifle and pack.

But he did for them both by his plan of attack.

OWEN:

Bent double, like old beggars under sacks,

Knock-kneed, coughing like hags, we cursed through
sludge,

Till on the haunting flares we turned our backs,

And towards our distant rest began to trudge.

Men marched asleep. Many had lost their boots,

But limped on, blood-shod. All went lame; all blind;

Drunk with fatigue; deaf even to the hoots

Of gas-shells dropping softly behind.

Gas! GAS! Quick, boys!—An ecstasy of fumbling

Fitting the clumsy helmets just in time,

But someone still was yelling out and stumbling

And flound'ring like a man in fire or lime.—

Dim through the misty panes and thick green light,

As under a green sea, I saw him drowning.

In all my dreams before my helpless sight,

He plunges at me, guttering, choking, drowning.

If in some smothering dreams, you too could pace

Behind the wagon that we flung him in,

And watch the white eyes writhing in his face,

His hanging face, like a devil's sick of sin;

If you could hear, at every jolt, the blood

Come gargling from the froth-corrupted lungs,

Obscene as cancer, bitter as the cud

Of vile, incurable sores on innocent tongues,—

My friend, you would not tell with such high zest

To children ardent for some desperate glory,

The old Lie: Dulce et decorum est

Pro patria mori.

DEATH, singing the first four lines to the tune of "My Love is Like a Red, Red Rose":

"Till a' ye see's gangrene, my boys,

A' ye see's gangrene,

And I will have ye here, my boys,

Where a' ye see's gangrene."

Thus the red rose burns and has for thee

The subtle stench of blasphemy,

And bell's chime

Is Hell's crime

And the bell tolls for thee. *[Pointing to Owen.]*

OWEN:

"O Jesus Christ! I'm hit," he said; and died.

Whether he vainly cursed or prayed indeed,

> The Bullets chirped—In vain, vain, vain!

> Machine-guns chuckled—Tut-tut! Tut-tut!

> And the Big Gun guffawed.

Another sighed,—"O Mother,—mother,—Dad!"

Then smiled at nothing, childlike, being dead.

> And the lofty Shrapnel-cloud

> Leisurely gestured,—Fool!

> And the splinters spat, and tittered.

"My Love!" one moaned. Love-languid seemed his
    mood,

Till slowly lowered, his whole face kissed the mud.

And the Bayonets' long teeth grinned;

Rabbles of Shells hooted and groaned;

And the Gas hissed.

DEATH sings slowly with a cold, sadistic sneer:

Pack up your troubles in your old kit-bag,

And smile, smile, smile,

While you've a lucifer to light your fag,

Smile, boys, that's the style.

What's the use of worrying?

It never was worth while, so

Pack up your troubles in your old kit-bag,

And smile, smile, smile.

Joseph Pearce

OWEN *[Rubs himself desperately as if frozen with cold]*:

Our brains ache, in the merciless iced east winds that
knife us . . .

Wearied we keep awake because the night is silent . . .

Low drooping flares confuse our memory of the salient
. . .

Worried by silence, sentries whisper, curious, nervous,

But nothing happens.

Watching, we hear the mad gusts tugging on the wire.

Like twitching agonies of men among its brambles.

Northward incessantly, the flickering gunnery rumbles,

Far off, like a dull rumour of some other war.

What are we doing here?

The poignant misery of dawn begins to grow . . .

We only know war lasts, rain soaks, and clouds sag
stormy.

Dawn massing in the east her melancholy army

Attacks once more in ranks on shivering ranks of gray,

> But nothing happens.

Sudden successive flights of bullets streak the silence.

Less deadly than the air that shudders black with snow,

With sidelong flowing flakes that flock, pause and
renew,

We watch them wandering up and down the wind's
nonchalance,

> But nothing happens.

Pale flakes with lingering stealth come feeling for our
faces—

We cringe in holes, back on forgotten dreams, and stare,
snow-dazed,

Deep into grassier ditches. So we drowse, sun-dozed,

Littered with blossoms trickling where the blackbird
fusses.

> Is it that we are dying?

Slowly our ghosts drag home: glimpsing the sunk fires
  glozed

With crusted dark-red jewels; crickets jingle there;

For hours the innocent mice rejoice: the house is theirs;

Shutters and doors all closed: on us the doors are
  closed—

  We turn back to our dying.

Since we believe not otherwise can kind fires burn;

Now ever suns smile true on child, or field, or fruit.

For God's invincible spring our love is made afraid;

Therefore, not loath, we lie out here; therefore were
  born,

  For love of God seems dying.

To-night, His frost will fasten on this mud and us,

Shrivelling many hands and puckering foreheads crisp.

The burying-party, picks and shovels in their shaking
  grasp,

Pause over half-known faces. All their eyes are ice,

But nothing happens.

Owen dies, crumpling to the floor.

DEATH:

And bell's chime

Is Hell's crime

And the bell tolls for thee: *[lifts Owen's face by the chin]*

A virgin child,

So weak and wild,

A lamb to the slaughter;

Blinking blind,

Fumbling find

And kiss the devil's daughter; *[kisses him]*

A debutant dilettante,

Into Hell to follow Dante

And dance the deadly dance . . .

[Death exits with Owen, leading him solemnly.]

SASSOON [watching in horror as Death departs with Owen]:

I knew a simple soldier boy

Who grinned at life in empty joy,

Slept soundly through the lonesome dark,

And whistled early with the lark.

In winter trenches, cowed and glum,

With crumps and lice and lack of rum,

He put a bullet through his brain.

No one spoke of him again.

You smug-faced crowds with kindling eye

Who cheer when soldier lads march by,

Sneak home and pray you'll never know

The hell where youth and laughter go.

Enter DEATH:

So they cheered as you marched to war,

A jingo jangled cavalier,

But sneered the sign above the door:

"Abandon hope who enters here."

And so Sassoon,

So soon, Sassoon,

In nightmare you're awake

With senseless insommeniacs,

Marneiacs, La Monsiacs,

A sight fair for a wake.

[Pauses. Turns. A look of sadness and anger on her face. Continues, addressing her words to Sassoon.]

The men that worked for England

They have their graves at home:

And bees and birds of England

About the cross can roam.

But they that fought for England,

Following a falling star,

Alas, alas for England

They have their graves afar.

And they that rule in England,

In stately conclave met,

Alas, alas for England,

They have no graves as yet.

SASSOON, angry, as if hearing Death's words:

THE boys came back. Bands played and flags were
flying,

And Yellow-Pressmen thronged the sunlit street

To cheer the soldiers who'd refrained from dying,

And hear the music of returning feet.

"Of all the thrills and ardours War has brought,

This moment is the finest." (So they thought.)

Snapping their bayonets on to charge the mob,

    Grim Fusiliers broke ranks with glint of steel,

At last the boys had found a cushy job.

I heard the Yellow-Pressmen grunt and squeal;

And with my trusty bombers turned and went

To clear those Junkers out of Parliament.

DEATH, *more calmly, looking at Sassoon:*

But the soldier is a mystic,

Foiling foolish fashion,

And redeemed and realistic,

Perceives poetic Passion;

And Siegfried freed

From Wagnerian curses

With sacred seed

Despair disperses.

SASSOON, *with a sad and somber solemnity:*

When you are standing at your hero's grave,

Or near some homeless village where he died,

Remember, through your heart's rekindling pride,

The German soldiers who were loyal and brave.

Men fought like brutes; and hideous things were done;

And you have nourished hatred, harsh and blind.

But in that Golgotha perhaps you'll find

The mothers of the men who killed your son.

[Cheering up, looking at the sky as if a weight has lifted from his shoulders. Continues joyfully, removing his army great-coat to reveal civilian clothes.]

My music-loving Self this afternoon

(Clothed in the gilded surname of Sassoon)

Squats in the packed Sheldonian and observes

An intellectual bee-hive perched and seated

In achromatic and expectant curves

Of buzzing, sunbeam-flecked, and overheated

Accommodation. Skins perspire . . . But hark! . . .

Begins the great B minor Mass of Bach.

The choir sings Gloria in excelsis Deo

With confident and well-conducted brio.

Outside, a motor-bike makes impious clatter,

Impinging on our Eighteenth-Century trammels.

God's periwigged: He takes a pinch of snuff.

The music's half-rococo . . . Does it matter

While those intense musicians shout the stuff

In Catholic Latin to the cultured mammals

Who agitate the pages of their scores? . . .

Meanwhile, in Oxford sunshine out of doors,

Birds in collegiate gardens rhapsodize

Antediluvian airs of worm-thanksgiving.

To them the austere and buried Bach replies

With song that from ecclesiasmus cries

Eternal Resurrexit to the living.

Hosanna in excelsis chants the choir

In pious contrapuntal jubilee.

Hosanna shrill the birds in sunset fire.

And Benedictus sings my heart to Me.

DEATH, *observing Sassoon:*

Upsurge surgery!

Open heart purgery

Puts perjury to flight,

And purgatorial seeking,

Falsehood forsaking,

Finds paradismal light!

[Pauses. Her face darkens. Sneers.]

April is the cruellest month, breeding

Lilacs out of the dead land, mixing

Memory and desire, stirring

Dull roots with spring rain.

Winter kept us warm, covering

Earth in forgetful snow, feeding

A little life with dried tubers.

[Pauses. Turns.]

What are the roots that clutch, what branches grow

Out of this stony rubbish? Son of man,

You cannot say, or guess, for you know only

A heap of broken images.

[Pauses. Turns. Points to Sassoon and then to the audience.]

I will show you something different from either

Your shadow at morning striding behind you

Or your shadow at evening rising to meet you;

I will show you fear in a handful of dust.

[Looks to the skies. The sound of aeroplanes and air raid sirens. Followed by explosions. Continues.]

Still falls the Rain—

Dark as the world of man, black as our loss—

Blind as the nineteen hundred and forty nails

Upon the Cross.

Still falls the Rain

With a sound like the pulse of the heart that is changed
    to the hammer-beat

In the Potter's Field, and the sound of the impious feet

On the Tomb:

Still falls the Rain

In the Field of Blood where the small hopes breed and
    the human brain

Nurtures its greed, that worm with the brow of Cain.

[A film of the explosion of an atomic bomb lights the backdrop to the stage, its mushroom cloud rising ominously over the actors.]

SASSOON *[Looking much older, stooped, with a stick.]*

In breaking of belief in human good;

In slavedom of mankind to the machine;

In havoc of hideous tyranny withstood,

And terror of atomic doom foreseen;

Deliver us from ourselves.

Chained to the wheel of progress uncontrolled;

World masterers with a foolish frightened face;

Loud speakers, leaderless and sceptic-souled;

Aeroplane angels, crashed from glory and grace;

Deliver us from ourselves.

In blood and bone contentiousness of nations,

And commerce's competitive re-start,

Armed with our marvellous monkey innovations,

And unregenerate still in head and heart;

Deliver us from ourselves.

[Kneels. Takes a Rosary from his pocket. Continues.]

Not properly Catholic, some might say, to like it best

When no one's in the cool white church that few
frequent

These sober-skied vocational afternoons in Lent.

There's sanctity in stillness, let it be confessed,

For one addicted much to meditationment—

This afternoon it seemed unconvert self came in,

Puzzled to perceive one at the altar rails, unminding;

Could this be he—hereafter offered him to win,

And faith revealed wheretoward he pilgrim'd without
finding?

How came it (ask your Angel—ask that vigilant voice)

That you this comfort found—that thus it grew to be

This close, child-minded calm? . . . Look those five
    candles lit

For five who have prayed your peace. (Candles were
    ever your choice

To tranquilize the mind, since boyhood.) They are what
    they are.

Two pennies for each. But Candlemas tells purity.

And we are told their innocent radiance will remit

Our errors. Although the lights of everlastingness,
    as someone said,

Can seem, for us poor souls, to dream so faint and far,

When at our broken orisons we kneel, unblessed,
    unbenefited.

While you were in your purgatorial time, you used to
    say

That though Creation's God remained so lost, such
    aeons away,

Somehow He would reveal Himself to you—some day!

For Him, the Living God, your soul and flesh could
    only cry aloud.

In watches of the night, when world event with
devildom went dark,

You implored illumination. But never being bowed

Obedient—never conceived an aureoled instance, an
assuring spark.

Outcast and unprotected contours of the soul,
Why in those hallowed minsters could they find no
home,
When nothing appeared more unpredictable than
this—your whole

Influence, relief, resultancy received from Rome?

[Pauses. Repeats a line pensively.]

Outcast and unprotected contours of the soul . . .

*[Gets to his feet, breaking off his prayer, and addresses the
audience directly.]*

"Outcast and unprotected contours of the soul" is not
my line. It's borrowed . . . Or stolen. No, "outcast and
unprotected contours of the soul" is not *me*, but beloved
Belloc. Hilaire *Belloc*. It must have been almost exactly
three years ago, when I was in the vortex of struggling
toward submission, that I came upon the following pas-
sage in a letter Belloc had written to a friend: "The

Faith, the Catholic Church, is discovered, is recognized, triumphantly enters reality like a landfall at sea which first was thought a cloud. The nearer it is seen, the more it is real, the less imaginary: the more direct and external its voice, the more indubitable its representative character, its 'persona,' its voice. The metaphor is not that men fall in love with it: the metaphor is that they discover home. 'This was what I sought. This was my need.' It is the very mould of the mind, the matrix to which corresponds in every outline the outcast and unprotected contour of the soul. It is Verlaine's 'Oh! Rome—oh! Mere!' Oh Rome! Oh Mother! And that not only to those who had it in childhood and have returned, but much more—and what a proof!—to those who come upon it from the hills of life and say to themselves, 'Here is the town.'"

Those lines of Belloc settled it for me. After reading them, I sat all afternoon, gazing out of the window, my mind a metaphysical reflection of a day of wild weather. My mind, my heart, my soul pervaded by a sort of ghostly climactic disturbance—cloud conflictings and murmurous intimations of spiritual debate. Questions asked . . . and answered. Belloc's magnificent words settled it, once and for all. "That's done it," I said to myself. My whole being was liberated. O that dear old Belloc could have known it before his death, or foreknown it when we met those many years ago.

Outcast and unprotected contours of the soul . . .

[Kneels. Returns to his prayer.]

Outcast and unprotected contours of the soul,

Why in those hallowed minsters could they find no
home,

When nothing appeared more unpredictable than
this—your whole

Influence, relief, resultancy received from Rome?

Look. Robed in white and blue, earth's best loved Lady
stands;

Mother Immaculate; name that shines to intercede.

Born on her birthday feast, until last year your hands

Kindled no candle, paid her heavenliness no heed.

Is it not well, that now you call yourself her child—

You and this rosary, at which—twelve months ago, you
might have shrugged and smiled?

This day twelve months ago—it was Ash Wednesday—
one

Mid-way between us two toward urgent hope fulfilled

Strove with submission. Arduous—forbidding—then
to meet

Inflexible Authority. While the work was willed,

The riven response from others to the task undone

Daunted a mind confused with ferment, incomplete:

There seemed so much renunciant consequence
involved,

When independent questioning self should yield,
indubitant and absolved.

This, then, brought our new making. Much emotional
stress—

Call it conversion: but the word can't cover such good.

It was like being in love with ambient blessedness—

In love with life transformed—life breathed afresh,
though yet half understood.

There had been many byways for the frustrate brain,

All leading to illusions lost and shrines forsaken . . .

One road before us now—one guidance for our gain—

One morning light—whatever the world's weather—
wherein wide-eyed to waken.

This is the time of year, when even for the old,

Youngness comes knocking on the heart with
undefined

Aches and announcements—blurred felicities foretold,

And (obvious utterance) wearying winter left behind.

I never felt it more than now, when out beyond these
safening walls

Sculptured with Stations of the Cross, spring-confident,
unburdened, bold,

The first March blackbird overheard to forward vision
flutes and calls.

You could have said this simple thing, old self, in any
previous year.

But not to that one ritual flame—to that all-answering
Heart abidant here.

DEATH:

And so Sassoon,

So soon, Sassoon,

You lurch triumphant,

And find the key

To liberty

From the search circumferent.

SASSOON *[Standing, stretching, looking up]:*

For grace in me divined

This metaphor I find:

A tree.

   How can that be?

This tree all winter through

Found no green work to do—

No life

   Therein ran rife.

But with an awoken year

What surge of sap is here—

What flood

    In branch and bud.

So grace in me can hide—

Be darkened and denied—

Then once again

    Vesture my every vein.

DEATH:

Upsurge surgery!

Open heart purgery

Puts perjury to flight,

And purgatorial seeking,

Falsehood forsaking,

Finds paradismal light!

SASSOON [*sickening, looking tired*]:

Bring no expectance of heaven unearned

No hunger for beatitude to be

Until the lesson of my life is learned

Through what Thou didst for me.

Bring no assurance of redeemed rest

No intimation of awarded grace

Only contrition, cleavingly confessed

To Thy forgiving face.

I ask one world of everlasting loss

In all I am, that other world to win.

My nothingness must kneel below Thy Cross.

There let new life begin.

[Sinks to his knees. Dies.]

DEATH*:*

And so Sassoon,

So soon, Sassoon,

You lurch triumphant,

And find the key

To liberty

From the search circumferent.

And as you turn the key

You learn to see

That it unlocks

The paradox

Of Paradise.

The chance to cease

Life's labour's test,

He grants you Peace,

Ite, missa est.

[Death lifts Sassoon by the hands. Sassoon stretches his rein-vigorated limbs. Taking Death's welcoming hand he follows her offstage.]

Finis.

We want to hear from you. Please send your comments about this book to us in care of zreview@zondervan.com. Thank you.